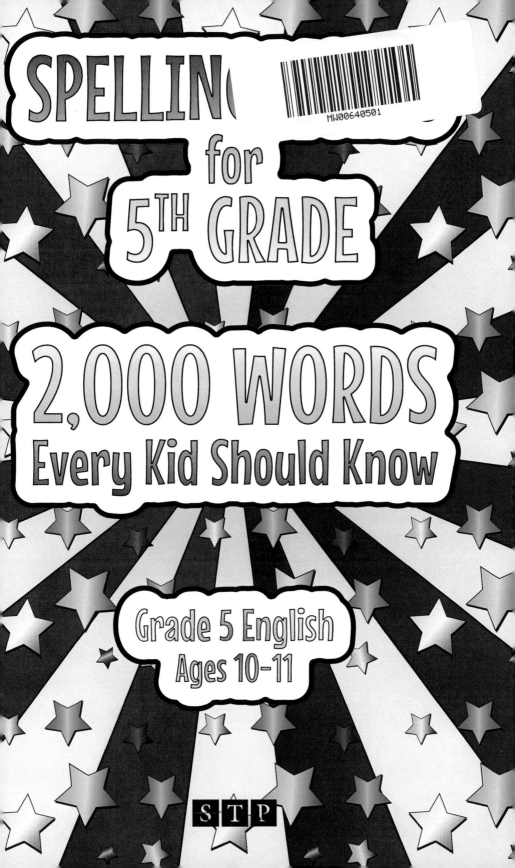

SPELLING for 5TH GRADE

2,000 WORDS
Every Kid Should Know

Grade 5 English
Ages 10-11

STP

ABOUT THIS BOOK

Using a **fresh approach** to spellings lists, this illustrated collection c
Spelling Words is designed **to make spelling fun** for your child whils
ensuring they master essential spelling rules by the end of Grade 5.

Containing **2,000** carefully selected **level-appropriate** words, this book i
made up of **70** Themed Spellings Lists that
- Have **brightly-colored illustrated backgrounds** and **engaging titles**
- Cover **loads of topics** that **actually interest kids** such as Dinosaurs, Ghosts, and TV
- Relate to other **areas covered at school** like geography, the Constitution, and recycling
- Target **key words that kids overuse** (e.g. 'look', 'fast', and 'big')
- Quietly introduce **specific areas of spelling** that kids need to know (e.g. using prefixes and suffixes, doubling consonants, and including silent letters)
- Are made up of **25 to 30 words each**

HOW TO USE IT

All the **lists are self-contained**, so you can work through them **in order**
or, you can dip in to use them for **focused practice**. And, as these lists ar
themed, they are **also a useful resource** for a range of **writing project
and exercises**.

For your convenience, an **Index** to the **spelling rules, patterns, an
themed areas** dealt with by each of the lists is included at the **back o
the book** on page 40.

Published by STP Books
An imprint of Swot Tots Publishing Ltd
Kemp House
152-160 City Road
London EC1V 2NX

www.swottotspublishing.com

Text, design, illustrations and layout © Swot Tots Publishing Ltd
First published 2020

Swot Tots Publishing Ltd have asserted their moral right under
the Copyright, Designs and Patents Act, 1988, to be identified
as the author of this work.

Typeset, cover design, and inside concept design by Swot Tc
Publishing Ltd.

British Library Cataloguing-in-Publication Data. A catalog
record for this book is available from the British Library.

ISBN 978-1-912956-31-9

CONTENTS

CONTENTS Cont.

Head-Scratchers

aural	council	metal
oral	counsel	mettle
bazaar	dual	naval
bizarre	duel	navel
boarders	eminent	sort
borders	imminent	sought
cast	foreword	suite
caste	forward	sweet
coarse	gorilla	taught
course	guerrilla	taut

Riddle Me This

baffle	enigma	ponder
bewilder	flummox	poser
brainteaser	hint	problematic
challenge	labyrinth	resolve
clue	maze	riddle
confound	muse	solve
confuse	mystery	stump
conundrum	mystify	unknown
crack	paradox	unravel
cryptic	perplex	untangle

Mamma Mia!

balcony	graffiti	quarantine
bandit	incognito	regatta
cappuccino	influenza	riviera
casino	lava	spaghetti
ciabatta	magenta	stiletto
confetti	malaria	tarantula
ducat	manifesto	terra-cotta
espresso	mustache	umbrella
extravaganza	pepperoni	vendetta
fresco	propaganda	vermicelli

Im- The Impossible

imbalance	impartial	imported
immaterial	impatient	imposed
immature	imperceptible	impossible
immigrate	imperil	impractical
immobile	impersonal	imprecise
immobilize	impersonated	imprisonment
immoral	implant	improbably
immortal	implausible	improper
immovable	implode	imprudent
impaired	impolite	impure

Burnt To A Crisp

arson	combustion	kindling
ashes	embers	roasted
blackened	firebug	scalded
blaze	flame	scorching
bonfire	furnace	searing
burn	glow	simmer
cauterized	hearth	singe
char	ignite	smolder
cinder	inferno	tinder
combustible	inflammable	wildfire

As Cold As Ice

Antarctic	frosty	icicle
Arctic	glacier	iciness
black ice	glittering	melting
block	hail	numbing
chilliness	harden	rime
chilly	ice cap	rink
cracking	ice cube	skating
crystal	iceberg	solidify
freeze	icebound	thaw
frost	icebox	tundra

Joining Forces I

backache	earthquake	scapegoat
backbone	fireworks	sidekick
backlog	forecast	skyscraper
bedrock	forefather	slapstick
blueprint	headquarters	spearmint
brainchild	household	stronghold
carefree	keystone	sunbath
commonplace	lifeblood	sweetmeat
commonwealth	lukewarm	wasteland
drawbridge	pinstripe	watchdog

Terrible Lizards

agile	feathered	quadruped
armor	fossil	remains
avian	fossilized	skeleton
carbon dating	herbivore	Triassic
carnivore	herd	vertebrate
Cretaceous	horned	
disappearance	Jurassic	
excavate	leviathan	
extinction	obliterate	
fearsome	prehistoric	

I Spy With My Little Eye

browse	inspect	regard
consider	investigate	review
contemplate	look	rubberneck
examine	monitor	scrutinize
focus	notice	seek
gape	observe	stare
gawk	peek	study
gaze	peep	survey
glance	peer	view
glimpse	peruse	watch

It's Not Rocket Science

analysis	empirical	objectivity
behavior	experiment	observation
breakthrough	experimental	organization
cause	experimentation	procedure
data	graph	proof
demonstration	hypothesis	research
development	laboratory	scientific
discipline	measurement	structure
discovery	measuring	systematic
effect	method	theory

Mapping The World

altitude	landscape	Plains
atlas	latitude	polar
climate	longitude	population
continent	meander	precipitation
contour	metropolis	rainfall
equator	mountains	soil
gradient	nation	subcontinent
hemisphere	ocean	terrain
landlocked	oceanic	tributary
landmass	physical features	Tropics

Happy Endings 1

auspicious	subconscious	pretentious
conscious	suspicious	repetitious
delicious	tenacious	scrumptious
ferocious	vicious	superstitious
gracious	voracious	vexatious
judicious	ambitious	
luscious	cautious	
malicious	fictitious	
precious	infectious	
precocious	nutritious	

Double Trouble

allergic	command	annihilate
ballerina	comment	anniversary
cellophane	commerce	antenna
collage	commit	cannibal
colleague	committee	cannon
dwelling	dilemma	colonnade
gazelle	immune	pennant
repellent	shimmer	personnel
satellite	summit	pinnacle
stallion	summon	tyranny

LION-HEARTED OR CHICKEN-LIVERED?

audacious	gutsy	fainthearted
bold	heroic	frightened
brave	intrepid	lily-livered
courageous	plucky	petrified
daredevil	resolute	scared
daring	stouthearted	terrified
dauntless	valiant	timorous
determined	cowardly	unheroic
doughty	craven	wimpy
fearless	dreading	yellow

Inside And Out

encased	personal	open-air
enclosed	private	outdoors
indoors	surrounded	outer
inner	walled	outermost
innermost	within	out-of-doors
interior	alfresco	outside
internal	beyond	outward
intrinsic	exterior	public
inward	external	surface
nuclear	extrinsic	without

In- The Incorrect

inability	incompatible	indistinct
inaccurate	incompetence	inedible
inactive	inconclusive	ineffective
inadequate	inconsiderate	inefficiency
inadvisable	inconsistency	ineligible
inanimate	inconsistent	inequality
inappropriate	incorrect	inexperience
inattentive	indefinable	infamous
inaudible	indefinite	inhumane
incapable	indirect	injustice

12

Silent, But Deadly

aisle	gnat	rendezvous
align	gnaw	salmon
asthma	indebted	scheme
beret	knuckle	scissors
chaos	mechanic	subtle
colonel	mnemonic	wrath
column	mortgage	wrestle
debris	pique	wretched
depot	plaque	wriggle
glisten	psalm	yacht

LOL!!!

cackle	hilarity	smile
chortle	howl	snicker
chuckle	hysterical	snigger
crack up	jocular	snort
deride	laugh	titter
gag	mirth	
giggle	mock	
grinning	peals	
guffaw	ridicule	
hilarious	roar	

Working Out

aerobics	judo	stretch
apparatus	leotard	therapeutic
athlete	locker	trainer
athletics	massage	training
biceps	membership	trampoline
coach	metabolism	treadmill
endurance	muscles	vault
exercise	physique	weights
fitness	sauna	workout
gymnasium	spandex	yoga

Happy Endings II

artificial	sacrificial	initial
beneficial	social	martial
crucial	special	palatial
especial	superficial	partial
facial	unofficial	potential
financial	celestial	residential
glacial	confidential	sequential
official	consequential	spatial
prejudicial	essential	tangential
provincial	influential	torrential

On Safari

breed	game warden	protection
conservation	grassland	ranger
diurnal	hunter	reservation
enclosure	lodge	safari
endangered	nocturnal	sanctuary
excursion	photography	savanna
exotic	poacher	solitary
expedition	predator	stalking
exploitation	preservation	stampede
extinct	prey	tracking

A Camping We Will Go

adventure	equipment	southern
backpack	flashlight	stove
campfire	hammock	tent
campground	hiking	trekking
campsite	northern	undergrowth
canoe	pitch	walking
clambering	raincoat	western
climbing	scenic	wilderness
compass	shelter	wildlife
eastern	sleeping bag	woodland

That Doesn't Look Right

accompany	disappear	physical
according	embarrass	prejudice
address	guarantee	queue
available	individual	restaurant
calendar	interrupted	secretary
community	medicine	separate
competition	necessary	strength
correspond	neighbor	temperature
desperate	ordinary	vegetable
determination	particular	vehicle

Greased Lightning

abruptly	galloping	snappily
accelerating	hastening	speedily
apace	hastily	sprightly
breakneck	lively	swiftly
briskly	posthaste	tearing
careering	promptly	
double-quick	quickly	
energetically	rapidly	
fleeting	rattling	
flying	rushing	

A Snail's Pace

crawling	languid	sluggish
creeping	leisurely	straggling
dawdling	lingering	tardy
deliberate	loitering	trailing
drifting	measured	unhurried
easing	plodding	
gradual	ponderous	
haltingly	shuffling	
inching	slothful	
lagging	slow-footed	

Il- The Illegible &
Ir- The Irresponsible

illegal	irredeemable	irresponsibly
illegality	irregular	irretrievable
illegally	irregularity	irreverence
illegible	irrelevance	irreverent
illegitimate	irrelevant	irreversible
illiteracy	irreparable	
illiterate	irreplaceable	
illogical	irresistible	
irrational	irresistibly	
irreconcilable	irresponsible	

The Root Of The Matter I

antebellum
antechamber
antedate
antemeridian
anteroom
aquamarine
aquaplane
aquarium
aquatic
autobiographies

autobiography
autocorrect
autograph
automate
automatic
automobiles
autonomous
autonomy
autopilot
autosave

circumference
circumflex
circumnavigate
circumscribe
circumvent

Mother Tongue

accent
articulate
bilingual
communication
diacritic
dialect
diction
fluency
formal
grammar

idiolect
idiom
informal
jargon
linguistic
multilingual
phonetic
polyglot
pronunciation
proverbial

regular
rhetoric
slang
speech
style
syllable
syntax
translation
vernacular
vocabulary

Native Speakers

Arabic	Hungarian	Portuguese
Bengali	Indonesian	Russian
Chinese	Italian	Spanish
Czech	Japanese	Swedish
Danish	Korean	Thai
Dutch	Mandarin	Tibetan
English	Norwegian	Turkish
French	Pashto	Urdu
Greek	Persian	Vietnamese
Hindi	Polish	Yoruba

Happy Endings 111

achievable	deniable	questionable
adorable	enviable	recommendable
answerable	favorable	regrettable
applicable	imaginable	respectable
appreciable	knowledgeable	supposable
attachable	likable	tolerable
breathable	mentionable	uncountable
changeable	persuadable	understandable
consumable	preventable	unforgettable
debatable	programmable	unreachable

Tuck In!

bolt	glut	stuff
breakfast	gorge	sup
chew	graze	swallow
consume	gulp	swig
cram	guzzle	swill
devour	have	
dine	munch	
eat	overeat	
feast	quaff	
feed	relish	

Spicing Things Up

allspice	fenugreek	vanilla
caraway	ginger	condiments
cardamom	juniper berries	flavoring
cayenne pepper	mustard seeds	powdered
chili pepper	nutmeg	seasoning
cinnamon	paprika	
cloves	peppercorns	
coriander seeds	saffron	
cumin	star anise	
fennel	turmeric	

Sage, Rosemary & Thyme

aloe vera	fennel	sage
basil	ginkgo	sorrel
bay leaves	lavender	tarragon
catnip	lemongrass	thyme
chamomile	marjoram	herbaceous
chervil	mint	
chickweed	nettle	
chives	oregano	
coriander	parsley	
dill	rosemary	

BOUQUETS OF FLOWERS

armada	convoy	stack
bouquet	fleet	string
bunch	fusillade	suit
bundle	library	suite
cache	pack	tuft
chest	quiver	
clump	ream	
cluster	set	
clutch	sheaf	
collection	squadron	

D Is For Danger

adverse	hazardous	powder keg
chancy	hostile	precarious
cliff-hanger	insecure	precipice
dangerous	jeopardy	risk
deadly	lethal	riskiness
dicey	menacing	threat
fatal	minefield	tinderbox
flash point	parlous	uncertain
hairy	peril	unsafe
hazard	perilous	unstable

What Was That Noise?

apparition	haunted	shadowy
aura	headless	souls
bodiless	illusion	specter
bogey	incorporeal	spectral
creepy	phantasm	spirit
daemon	phantom	spook
ectoplasm	poltergeist	spooky
eerie	revenant	sprite
ghostly	scary	vision
ghoul	séance	wraith

ABRACADABRA!

abracadabra	familiar	sorcerer
beldam	foretell	sorceress
black magic	hag	sorcery
broomstick	hex	spell
chant	hocus-pocus	voodoo
charm	jinx	warlock
conjurer	magician	witch
crone	magus	witchcraft
curse	necromancy	wizard
enchantress	predict	wizardry

And Then...And Then...

additionally	initially	secondly
altogether	lastly	specifically
conversely	likewise	thirdly
equally	moreover	unlike
fifthly	nonetheless	whereas
finally	notably	
firstly	obviously	
fourthly	overall	
including	particularly	
indeed	regardless	

When In Rome...

accelerate	cordial	hostility
agriculture	corollary	lagoon
ambiguous	culinary	lateral
animate	culpable	linear
astute	deity	lucrative
aviation	dulcet	luxury
benefactor	duration	medium
centurion	endorse	peninsula
commentary	equestrian	privilege
condone	exasperate	procure

True Or False?

artless	simple	devious
blunt	sincere	double-dealing
candid	straight	false
direct	straightforward	hypocritical
forthright	truthful	insincere
frank	cheating	lying
honest	crafty	sly
open	cunning	sneaky
outspoken	deceitful	treacherous
plain	deceptive	untruthful

Happy Endings IV

accessible	divisible	legible
admissible	edible	permissible
audible	eligible	plausible
collapsible	flexible	possible
collectible	forcible	reprehensible
compatible	inadmissible	reversible
constructible	indivisible	suggestible
credible	intangible	susceptible
deducible	invincible	tangible
destructible	invisible	visible

Save The Planet

alternative energy	eco-friendly	greenhouse gas
biodegradable	ecosystem	nonrenewable
biodiversity	emissions	ozone layer
biohazard	environmentalist	pollution
climate change	extermination	preserve
compostable	fallout	renewable
contaminate	fauna	surroundings
decimation	flora	sustainable
deforestation	global warming	toxic waste
desertification	greenhouse effect	unsustainable

GOING GREEN

biowaste	garbage	sorting
by-product	incineration	sustainability
cardboard	landfill	toxicity
compost	organic	trash
convert	packaging	treatment
decompose	plastic	
discarded	recycle	
disposal	reprocess	
environmental	repurpose	
fertilizers	rubbish	

Near And Far

adjacent	local	far-flung
adjoining	nearby	farthest
alongside	neighboring	furthest
around	next-door	inaccessible
attached	together	isolated
beside	afar	lonely
central	apart	outlying
close	distant	outermost
handy	extreme	remote
immediate	faraway	removed

ALL AT SEA

ahoy	fathom	offshore
anchor	harbor	paddle
astern	helm	porthole
bow	launch	prow
buoy	lifeboat	rescue
cabin	lighthouse	rigging
coast guard	mainsail	rudder
coastal	mooring	seabed
cruise	nautical	tiller
disembark	oar	voyage

All Aboard!

bullet train	high-speed	shunt
cargo	intercity	sleeping car
commuter	locomotive	station
commuter train	main line	subway
diesel	monorail	ticket
electric	passenger	timetable
engine	passenger coach	track
express	rail carrier	transit
fare	railroad	transportation
freight	round-trip	tunnel

Grrrrrr!

aggravate	harass	rankle
anger	incense	ruffle
annoy	infuriate	tease
antagonize	irk	trouble
bother	irritate	vex
displease	madden	
disturb	nag	
enrage	pester	
gall	plague	
goad	provoke	

As Big As An Elephant

astronomical	extensive	prodigious
behemoth	gigantic	sizable
bulky	huge	spacious
bumper	humongous	substantial
cavernous	immense	titanic
colossal	infinite	towering
considerable	juggernaut	tremendous
cumbersome	large	vast
elephantine	massive	voluminous
enormous	outsize	whopping

ON THE SMALL SIDE

atomic
bite-size
cramped
diminutive
dinky
infinitesimal
insubstantial
itty-bitty
lilliputian
limited

little
mini
miniature
minuscule
minute
modest
negligible
pint-size
pocket-size
poky

small
teensy
teeny
tiny
undersized

Oodles Of Ologies

anthropology
archaeology
astrology
biology
chronology
cosmology
criminology
etymology
geology
ideology

meteorology
methodology
microbiology
nanotechnology
neurology
paleontology
pharmacology
physiology
psychology
radiology

sociology
technology
terminology
theology
zoology

Happy Endings V

abundance	distance	insurance
alliance	elegance	nuisance
allowance	entrance	observance
annoyance	fragrance	radiance
arrogance	grievance	relevance
assistance	guidance	reliance
assurance	hesitance	substance
brilliance	hindrance	surveillance
clearance	ignorance	tolerance
defiance	instance	vengeance

TUTANKHAMEN & CO.

ankh	flooding	pyramids
artifacts	hieroglyphics	reliefs
bureaucracy	irrigation	rituals
cataract	kingdom	ruins
civilization	lapis lazuli	sarcophagus
delta	mastaba	scribe
discoveries	mummification	silt
dynasties	obelisks	sphinx
empire	papyrus	unification
excavation	pharaoh	worshipping

As Cool As A Cucumber

calm	placid	undismayed
collected	poised	unemotional
comfortable	relaxed	unexcited
composed	sedate	unfazed
cool	self-possessed	unflustered
easygoing	serene	unmoved
level	settled	unperturbed
mellow	tranquil	unruffled
nonchalant	unbothered	untroubled
peaceful	unconcerned	unworried

On Edge

agitated	edgy	shaken
alarmed	flustered	tense
anxious	fretful	troubled
apprehensive	jittery	twitchy
bothered	jumpy	uncomfortable
concerned	nervous	uneasy
disconcerted	panicked	unnerved
dismayed	perturbed	unsettled
distracted	rattled	uptight
disturbed	ruffled	worried

A Is for Amazing

amazing	great	sensational
astonishing	incredible	spectacular
astounding	inspirational	staggering
awesome	lovely	stupendous
breathtaking	magnificent	sublime
excellent	marvelous	super
fabulous	mind-blowing	superb
fantastic	outstanding	swell
glorious	phenomenal	terrific
gorgeous	remarkable	wonderful

The Root Of The Matter 11

hyperactive	microcosm	polyester
hypercompetitive	microdot	polyethylene
hypercritical	microfiber	polygon
hyperlink	microfilm	polygraph
hypersensitive	micromanage	polymath
hypertext	microorganism	
hyperventilate	microphone	
macrocosm	microscopic	
microchip	microsurgery	
microcomputer	microwave	

Both Sides Of The Coin I

careful	trusty	reckless
conscientious	unfaltering	unconscientious
dependable	careless	undependable
meticulous	heedless	unreliable
reliable	ill-considered	untrustworthy
responsible	incautious	
sensible	neglectful	
sound	negligent	
steady	precipitous	
trustworthy	rash	

We The People

amendment	executive	minority rights
articles	federal	parchment
Bill of Rights	federalism	president
citizenry	freedoms	ratification
civil rights	judicial	responsibilities
codified	justice	safeguard
confederation	legislative	Senate
Congress	legislature	signatories
constitution	liberty	Supreme Court
equality	majority rule	vice president

Happy Endings VI

absence	essence	prudence
adolescence	evidence	recurrence
audience	existence	reference
convenience	influence	residence
convergence	innocence	resilience
correspondence	insolence	science
dependence	lenience	sentence
difference	obedience	sequence
disobedience	patience	silence
eloquence	presence	violence

What Are You Feeling?

admiration	euphoria	misery
agitation	gratitude	nervousness
anxiety	grief	pain
boredom	guilt	pleasure
despair	happiness	pride
disappointment	heartache	regret
disbelief	homesickness	sadness
embarrassment	jealousy	surprise
enjoyment	joy	wonder
envy	merriment	worry

Both Sides Of The Coin II

efficient
kempt
methodical
neat
ordered
orderly
organized
shipshape
spruce
tidy

uncluttered
chaotic
cluttered
disheveled
disorderly
disorganized
inefficient
jumbled
messy
muddled

ramshackle
rumpled
scruffy
unkempt
untidy

And The Orchestra Played...

arpeggios
bar
baton
brass
choir
classical
clef
composer
conductor
conservatory

harmony
libretto
melody
notation
octet
opera
orchestral
percussion
quartet
rehearsal

scales
sheet music
solo
soloist
sonata
staff
strings
symphony
treble clef
woodwind

Music To My Ears

accordion	guitar	recorder
bagpipes	harp	saxophone
banjo	keyboard	sitar
bassoon	lute	tambourine
castanets	lyre	timpani
cello	mandolin	trombone
clarinet	oboe	trumpet
double bass	organ	tuba
flute	piano	viola
French horn	piccolo	violin

JOINING FORCES II

big-boned	heavy-duty	long-lived
big-time	heavy-handed	long-lost
broken-down	high-class	short-lived
die-hard	high-definition	short-tempered
four-dimensional	high-end	short-term
four-letter	high-octane	thick-skinned
hard-and-fast	ice-cold	thin-skinned
hard-boiled	large-hearted	tight-knit
hard-earned	light-headed	tight-lipped
hard-won	long-lasting	tight-mouthed

The Small Screen

anchorperson	drama	program
broadcast	episode	ratings
buffering	footage	satellite dish
bulletin	game show	screen
call-in	live	season
channel	miniseries	sitcom
commercial	movie	streaming
docudrama	news flash	talk show
documentary	newscaster	update
downloading	pilot	viewer

Greeks Bearing Gifts

academy	catastrophe	ethic
aesthetic	ceramic	eucalyptus
agony	chrome	galaxy
ambrosia	chrysalis	gastric
amphibian	cyan	hypodermic
antidote	demographic	nostalgia
architect	diagram	orthodox
arctic	energetic	parallel
aristocracy	epoch	problem
cardiac	ether	symbol

Are These Clean Or Dirty?

clean	unblemished	grubby
cleansed	unpolluted	mucky
hygienic	unsoiled	muddy
laundered	unstained	polluted
pure	washed	soiled
purified	blemished	stained
sanitary	contaminated	unclean
spotless	filthy	unhygienic
sterile	greasy	unpurified
sterilized	grimy	unwashed

CHILLAXING!

absorbing	enthusiast	pursuit
activity	escapism	recreation
amateur	fascinating	relaxation
amusement	game	satisfying
collecting	hobbies	sport
craze	indulgence	
creative	interest	
distraction	leisure	
diversion	obsession	
enjoyable	pastime	

V Is For Vile

abhorrent	grim	nightmarish
appalling	grisly	outrageous
atrocious	gruesome	shocking
bloodcurdling	harrowing	spine-chilling
dire	hideous	terrible
distressing	horrendous	terrifying
dreadful	horrible	tragic
fearful	horrid	unpleasant
frightful	horrific	unspeakable
ghastly	horrifying	vile

ZZZZZZ...

asleep	insomnia	sleepwalking
catnap	late-night	sleepyhead
daydream	nap	slumber
doze	nightmare	slumberous
dreamless	nod off	snooze
drift	oversleep	snore
drowse	repose	undisturbed
drowsy	rest	wakeful
forty winks	shut-eye	wakefulness
hibernate	siesta	weariness

INDEX

Made in United States
North Haven, CT
24 September 2024